Assessment in Health Professions Education

The health professions, i.e., persons engaged in teaching, research, administration, and/or testing of students and professionals in medicine, dentistry, nursing, pharmacy, and other allied health fields, have never had a comprehensive text devoted specifically to their assessment needs.

Assessment in Health Professions Education is the first comprehensive text written specifically for this audience. It presents assessment fundamentals and their theoretical underpinnings, and covers specific assessment methods. Although scholarly and evidence-based, the book is accessible to non-specialists.

- This is the first text to provide comprehensive coverage of assessment in the health professions. It can serve as a basic textbook in introductory and intermediate assessment and testing courses, and as a reference book for graduate students and professionals.
- Although evidence-based, the writing is keyed to consumers of measurement topics and data rather than to specialists. Principles are presented at the intuitive level without statistical derivations.
- Validity evidence is used as an organizing theme. It is presented early (Chapter 2) and referred to throughout.

Steven M. Downing (PhD, Michigan State University) is Associate Professor of Medical Education at the University of Illinois at Chicago and is the Principal Consultant at Downing & Associates. Formerly he was Director of Health Programs and Deputy Vice President at the National Board of Medical Examiners and Senior Psychometrician at the American Board of Internal Medicine.

Rachel Yudkowsky (MD, Northwestern University Medical School, MHPE, University of Illinois at Chicago) is Assistant Professor of Medical Education at the University of Illinois at Chicago. She has been director of the Dr. Allan L. and Mary L. Graham Clinical Performance Center since 2000, where she develops standardized patient and simulation-based programs for the instruction and assessment of students, residents, and staff.

Assessment in Health Professions Education

Edited by
Steven M. Downing, PhD
Rachel Yudkowsky, MD MHPE

Routledge
Taylor & Francis Group

NEW YORK AND LONDON

First published 2009
by Routledge
270 Madison Ave, New York, NY 10016

Simultaneously published in the UK
by Routledge
2 Park Square, Milton Park, Abingdon, Oxon OX14 4RN

Routledge is an imprint of the Taylor & Francis Group, an informa business

© 2009 Taylor and Francis

Typeset in Caslon by Swales & Willis Ltd, Exeter, Devon
Printed and bound in the United States of America on acid-free paper by
Edwards Brothers, Inc.

Library of Congress Cataloging-in-Publication Data
Assessment in health professions education / edited by Steven M. Downing,
Rachel Yudkowsky.
    p. ; cm.
Includes bibliographical references and index.
1. Medicine—Study and teaching. 2. Educational tests and measurements.
I. Downing, Steven M. II. Yudkowsky, Rachel.
[DNLM: 1. Health Occupations—education. 2. Educational Measurement—
methods. W 18 A83443 2009]
R834.5.A873 2009
610.71—dc22

2008042218

ISBN 10: 0–8058–6127–0 (hbk)
ISBN 10: 0–8058–6128–9 (pbk)
ISBN 10: 0–203–88013–7 (ebk)

ISBN 13: 978–0–8058–6127–3 (hbk)
ISBN 13: 978–0–8058–6128–0 (pbk)
ISBN 13: 978–0–203–88013–5 (ebk)

To my husband Moshe
Looking forward to the next billion seconds and more

To our children Eliezer and Channah
Who bring us much pride and joy

And in memory of our son Yehuda Nattan
May his memory be a blessing to all who loved him

~ RY

Contents

List of Figures

List of Tables

Preface

The purpose of this book is to present a basic yet comprehensive treatment of assessment methods for use by health professions educators. While there are many excellent textbooks in psychometric theory and its application to large-scale standardized testing programs and many educational measurement and assessment books designed for elementary and secondary teachers and graduate students in education and psychology, none of these books is entirely appropriate for the specialized educational and assessment requirements of the health professions. Such books lack essential topics of critical interest to health professions educators and may contain many chapters that are of little or no interest to those engaged in education in the health professions.

Assessment in Health Professions Education presents chapters on the fundamentals of testing and assessment together with some of their theoretical and research underpinnings plus chapters devoted to specific assessment methods used widely in health professions education. Although scholarly, evidence-based and current, this book is intended to be readable, understandable, and practically useful for the non-measurement specialist. Validity evidence is an organizing theme and is the conceptual framework used throughout the chapters of this book, because the editors and authors think that all assessment data require some amount of scientific evidence to support or refute the intended interpretations of the assessment data and that validity is the single most important attribute of all assessment data.

The Fundamentals

Chapters 1 to 6 present some of the theoretical fundamentals of assessment, from the special perspective of the health professions educator. These chapters are basic and fairly non-technical but are intended to provide health professions instructors some of the essential background needed to understand, interpret, develop, and successfully apply many of the specialized assessment methods or techniques discussed in Chapters 7 to 12.

In Chapter 1, Downing and Yudkowsky present a broad overview of assessment in the health professions. This chapter provides the basic concepts and language of assessment and orients the reader to the conceptual framework for this book. The reader who is unfamiliar with the jargon of assessment or is new to health professions education will find this chapter a solid introduction and orientation to the basics of this specialized discipline.

Chapter 2 (Downing & Haladyna) discusses validity and the classic threats to validity for assessment data. Validity encompasses all other topics in assessment and thus this chapter is placed early in the book to emphasize its importance. Validity is the organizing principle of this book, so the intention of this chapter is to provide readers with the interpretive tools needed to apply this concept to all other topics and concepts discussed in later chapters.

Chapters 3 and 4 both concern reliability of assessment data, with Chapter 3 (Axelson & Kreiter) discussing the general principles and common applications of reliability. In Chapter 4, Kreiter presents the fundamentals of an important special type of reliability analysis, Generalizability Theory, and applies this methodology to health professions education.

In Chapter 5, Downing presents some basic information on the statistics of testing, discussing the fundamental score unit, standard scores, item analysis, and some information and examples of practical hand-calculator formulas used to evaluate test and assessment data in typical health professions education settings.

Standard setting or the establishment of passing scores is the topic presented by Yudkowsky, Downing, and Tekian in Chapter 6.

Defensibility of absolute passing scores—as opposed to relative or normative passing score methods—is the focus of this chapter, together with many examples provided for some of the most common methods utilized for standard setting and some of the statistics used to evaluate those standards.

The Methods

The second half of the book—Chapters 7 to 12—cover all the basic methods commonly used in health professions education settings, starting with written tests of cognitive knowledge and achievement and proceeding through chapters on observational assessment, performance examinations, simulations, oral exams and portfolio assessment. Each of these topics represents an important method or technique used to measure knowledge and skills acquisition of students and other learners in the health professions.

In Chapter 7, Downing presents an overview of written tests of cognitive knowledge. Both constructed-response and selected-response formats are discussed, with practical examples and guidance summarized from the research literature. Written tests of all types are prevalent, especially in classroom assessment settings in health professions education. This chapter aims to provide the instructor with the basic knowledge and skills needed to effectively test student learning.

Chapter 8, written by McGaghie and colleagues, overviews observational assessment methods, which may be the most prevalent assessment method utilized, especially in clinical education settings. The fundamentals of sound observational assessment methods are presented and recommendations are made for ways to improve these methods.

Yudkowsky discusses performance examinations in Chapter 9. This chapter provides the reader with guidelines for performance assessment using techniques such as standardized patients and Objective Structured Clinical Exams (OSCEs). These methods are extremely useful in skills testing, which is generally a major objective of clinical education and training at all levels of health professions education.

High-tech simulations used in assessment are the focus of Chapter 10, by McGaghie and Issenberg. Simulation technology is becoming ever more important and useful for teaching and assessment, especially in procedural disciplines such as surgery. This chapter presents the state-of-the art for simulations and will provide the reader with the tools needed to begin to understand and use these methods effectively.

Chapters 11 and 12, written by Tekian and Yudkowsky, provide basic information on the use of oral examinations and portfolios. Oral exams in various forms are used widely in health professions education worldwide. This chapter provides information on the fundamental strengths and limitations of the oral exam, plus some suggestions for improving oral exam methods. Portfolio assessment, discussed in Chapter 12, is both old and new. This method is currently enjoying a resurgence in popularity and is widely applied in all levels of health professions education. This chapter presents basic information that is useful to those who employ this methodology.

Acknowledgments

As is often the case in specialized books such as this, the genesis and motivation to edit and produce the book grew out of our teaching and faculty mentoring roles. We have learned much from our outstanding students in the Masters of Health Professions Education (MHPE) program at the University of Illinois at Chicago (UIC) and we hope that this book provides some useful information to future students in this program and in the many other health professions education graduate and faculty development programs worldwide.

We are also most grateful to all of our authors, who dedicated time from their over-busy professional lives to make a solid contribution to assessment in health professions education.

We thank Lane Akers, our editor/publisher, at Routledge, for his encouragement of this book and his patience with our much delayed writing schedule. We also wish to acknowledge and thank all our reviewers. Their special expertise, insight, and helpful comments have made this a stronger publication.

Brittany Allen, at UIC, assisted us greatly in the final preparation of this book and we are grateful for her help. We also thank our families, who were most patient with our many distractions over the long time-line required to produce this book.

Steven M. Downing
Rachel Yudkowsky
University of Illinois at Chicago, College of Medicine
July 2008

Chapter-specific Acknowledgments

Chapter 2 Acknowledgments

This chapter is a modified and expanded version of two papers which appeared in the journal, *Medical Education*. The full references are:

Downing, S.M. (2003). Validity: On the meaningful interpretation of assessment data. *Medical Education*, 37, 830–837.
Downing, S.M., & Haladyna, T.M. (2004). Validity threats: Overcoming interference with proposed interpretations of assessment data. *Medical Education*, 38, 327–333.

Chapter 5 Acknowledgments

The author is grateful to Clarence D. Kreiter, PhD for his review of this chapter and helpful suggestions.

Chapter 6 Acknowledgments

This chapter is an updated and expanded version of a paper that appeared in *Teaching and Learning in Medicine* in 2006:

Downing, S., Tekian, A., & Yudkowsky, R. (2006). Procedures for establishing defensible absolute passing scores on performance examinations in health professions education. *Teaching and Learning in Medicine*, 18(1), 50–57.

The authors are grateful to the publishers Taylor and Francis for permission to reproduce here material from the paper. The original paper is available at the journal's website www.informaworld.com.

Chapter 7 Acknowledgments

The author is most grateful to Thomas M. Haladyna, PhD for his review of and constructive criticisms and suggestions for this chapter.

Chapter 12 Acknowledgments

Our thanks to Mark Gelula, PhD for reviewing this chapter and for his helpful comments and suggestions.

1

Introduction to Assessment in the Health Professions

Steven M. Downing and Rachel Yudkowsky

Assessment is defined by the *Standards for Educational and Psychological Testing* (AERA, APA, & NCME, 1999, p. 172) as: "Any systematic method of obtaining information from tests and other sources, used to draw inferences about characteristics of people, objects, or programs." This is a broad definition, but it summarizes the scope of this book, which presents current information about both assessment theory and its practice in health professions education. The focus of this book is on the assessment of learning and skill acquisition in *people*, with a strong emphasis on broadly defined achievement testing, using a variety of methods.

Health professions education is a specialized discipline comprised of many different types of professionals, who provide a wide range of health care services in a wide variety of settings. Examples of health professionals include physicians, nurses, pharmacists, physical therapists, dentists, optometrists, podiatrists, other highly specialized technical professionals such as nuclear and radiological technicians, and many other professionals who provide health care or health related services to patients or clients. The most common thread uniting the health professions may be that all such professionals must complete highly selective educational courses of study, which usually include practical training as well as classroom instruction; those who successfully complete these rigorous courses of study have the serious responsibility of taking care of patients—sometimes in life and death situations. Thus health professionals usually require a specialized license or other type of certificate to practice. It is important to base our health professions education assessment practices and methods on the best research evidence available, since many of the decisions made about our students ultimately have impact on health care delivery outcomes for patients.

The *Standards* (AERA, APA, & NCME, 1999) represent the consensus opinion concerning all major policies, practices, and issues in assessment. This document, revised every decade or so, is sponsored by the three major North American professional associations concerned with assessment and its application and practice: The American Educational Research Association (AERA), the American Psychological Association (APA), and the National Council on Measurement in Education (NCME). The *Standards* will be referenced frequently in this book because they provide excellent guidance based on the best contemporary research evidence and the consensus view of educational measurement professionals.

This book devotes chapters to both the contemporary theory of assessment in the health professions and to the practical methods typically used to measure students' knowledge acquisition and their abilities to perform in clinical settings. The theory sections apply to nearly all measurement settings and are essential to master for those who wish to practice sound, defensible, and meaningful assessments of their health professions students. The methods section deals specifically with common procedures or techniques used in health professions education—written tests of cognitive achievement, observational methods typically used for clinical assessment, and performance examinations such as standardized patient examinations.

George Miller's Pyramid

Miller's pyramid (Miller, 1990) is often cited as a useful model or taxonomy of knowledge and skills with respect to assessment in health professions education. Figure 1.1 reproduces the Miller pyramid, showing schematically that cognitive knowledge is at the base of a pyramid upon which foundation all other important aspects or features of learning in the health professions rests. This is the "knows" level of essential factual knowledge, the knowledge of biological pro-cess and scientific principles on which most of the more complex learn-ings rest. Knowledge is the essential prerequisite for most all other types of learning expected of our students. Miller would likely agree that this "knows" level is best measured by written objective tests, such as selected- and constructed-response tests. The "knows how" level of the Miller pyramid adds a level of complexity to the cognitive scheme, indicating something more than simple recall or recognition of fac-tual knowledge. The "knows how" level indicates a student's ability to manipulate knowledge in some useful way, to apply this knowledge, to be able to demonstrate some understanding of the relationships between concepts and principles, and may even indicate the student's ability to describe the solution to some types of novel problems. This level can also be assessed quite adequately with carefully crafted writ-ten tests, although some health professions educators would tend to use other methods, such as oral exams or other types of more subject-ive, observational procedures. The "knows how" level deals with cog-nitive knowledge, but at a somewhat more complex or higher level than the "knows" level. The first two levels of the Miller pyramid are concerned with knowledge that is verbally mediated; the emphasis is on verbal-type knowledge and the student's ability to describe this knowledge verbally rather than on "doing."

The "shows how" level moves the methods of assessment toward performance methods and away from traditional written tests of know-ledge. Most performance-type examinations, such as using simulated patients to assess the communication skills of medical students, dem-onstrate the "shows how" level of the Miller pyramid. All such per-formance exams are somewhat artificial, in that they are presented in a standard testing format under more-or-less controlled conditions. Specific cases or problems are pre-selected for testing and special "standardized patients" are selected and trained to portray the case and rate the student's performance using checklists and/or rating scales. All these standardization procedures add to the measurement qualities of the assessment, but may detract somewhat from the authenticity of the assessment. Miller's "does" level indicates the highest level of assessment, associated with more independent and free-range observations of the student's performance in actual patient or clinical settings. Some standardization and control of the assessment setting and situation is traded for complete, uncued authenticity of assessment. The student brings together all the cognitive knowledge, skills, abilities, and experience into a performance in the real world, which is observed by expert and experienced clinical teachers and raters.

Miller's pyramid can be a useful construct to guide our thinking about teaching and assessment in the health professions. However, many other systems or taxonomies of knowledge structure are also discussed in the literature. For example, one of the oldest and most frequently used taxonomies of cognitive knowledge (the "knows" and "knows how" level for Miller) is Bloom's Cognitive Taxonomy (Bloom, Engelhart, Furst, Hill, & Krathwohl, 1956). The Bloom Cognitive Taxonomy ranks knowledge from very simple recall or recognition of facts to higher levels of synthesizing and evaluating factual knowledge and solving novel problems. The Bloom cognitive taxonomy, which is often used to guide written testing, is discussed more thoroughly in Chapter 7. For now, we suggest that for meaningful and successful assessments, there must be some rational system or plan to

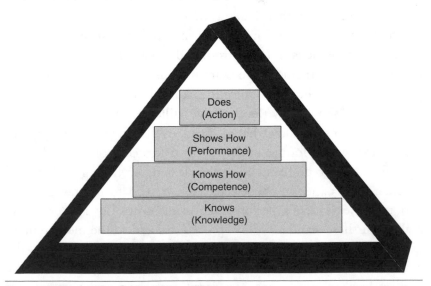

Figure 1.1 George Miller's Pyramid (Miller, 1990).

connect the content tested to the knowledge, skills and abilities that we think important for learning.

Four Major Assessment Methods

In health professions education, almost all of the assessments we construct, select, and administer to our students can be classified into one (or more) of these four categories: Written tests, performance tests, clinical observational methods, and a broad "miscellaneous" category consisting of many other types of assessments, such as oral examinations ("vivas" or live patient exams in the classic long and short-cases), portfolios, chart-stimulated recall type assessments, and so on. These methods fit, more or less, with the Miller Pyramid shown in Figure 1.1. This section provides an overview of these methods, each of which will be considered in detail in other chapters.

Written Tests

Most of the formal assessment in health professions education includes some type of written testing. This simply means that the tests consist of written questions or stimuli, to which students or trainees must respond. There are two major types of written tests: Constructed-response (CR) tests and selected-response (SR) tests. Both of these formats can be presented in either the traditional paper-and-pencil format or in the newer computer-based formats, in which computer screens are used to present the test stimuli and record examinee responses or answers. For constructed-response tests, questions or stimuli are presented and examinees respond by writing or typing responses or answers. There are many varieties of constructed-response formats, including "fill-in-the-blanks" type items and short- and long-answer essays. Selected-response tests, on the other hand, present a question or stimulus (referred to as a stem), followed by a number of option choices. The multiple-choice (MC) item is the prototype for selected-response formats, but there are many variations on the theme, such as true-false and alternate-choice items, matching items, extended matching items, and many other innovative formats (Sireci & Zenisky, 2006) used primarily in computer-based tests (CBTs). While the constructed-response format is probably the most widely used worldwide, the selected-response format is the true "workhorse" of the testing world, especially in North America. This format has many practical advantages and at least 90 years of research to support its validity (Downing, 2002; Welch, 2006). Chapter 7 discusses both constructed and selected response written tests.

Observational of Clinical Performance

Assessment of clinical performance during clinical training is a very common form of assessment in health professions education. These types of assessment range from informal observations of students in clinical settings to very formal (and sometimes complex) systems of data gathering from multiple raters about the performance of health professions students in actual clinical settings, with real patients over lengthy periods of time. Typically, many of these observational assessment methods rely on checklists and rating forms, completed by faculty and other instructors in clinical settings.

Many of these observational assessments carry major weight in overall or composite grading schemes, such that the stakes associated with these observations of clinical behavior are high for the student. Health professions educators rely heavily on these types of observational assessments, but the shortcomings of these methods are well known and are difficult to remediate (e.g., Williams, Klamen, & McGaghie, 2003). Validity problems are common in data obtained from observational methods, yet these methods are highly valued in health professions education because of strong traditions and (often false) beliefs concerning the quality of the data obtained. Chapter 8 is devoted to a discussion of the issues concerning assessments based on observation of clinical performance in real-life settings and Chapter 12 discusses other types of observational methods in the context of portfolios, noting their strengths and limitations.

Performance Tests

The term "performance test" is the generic term used to describe many types of formal testing with the primary purpose of measuring "what students can do," rather than simply "what they know." Health professions education has always valued the assessment of student performance, with a traditional reliance on "live patient oral examinations," and so-called "vivas," during which students were orally questioned in the classic long and short cases. Systematic, formal performance testing began fairly recently, with the introduction of the Objective Structured Clinical Examination (OSCE) by Hart and Harden in the late 1970s (e.g., Harden, Stevenson, Downie, & Wilson, 1975). Medical education in particular has adopted performance testing at all levels of training, from early in the medical school curriculum through graduate or residency training, including its use as one component of the United States Medical Licensure Examination (NBME, 2006) and post-graduate licensure examinations in Canada (Medical Council of Canada).

For simplicity, we categorize simulations as a type of performance examination, but many authors and researchers classify all types of simulations, used for both teaching and assessment, as a separate category. The term "simulation" refers to a testing method that utilizes a representation of a real-world task. Simulations cover a wide-range of methods and modalities, from fairly simple structured oral exams to very sophisticated and intricate computer simulations of complex patient clinical cases such as Primum® Computer-Based Case Simulations (CCS), one component of the United States Medical Licensure Examination (USMLE) Step II medical licensing test (NBME, 2006). Simulated or standardized patient exams, often used in OSCE stations, are utilized for both teaching and assessment and now comprise a major category of performance testing in many areas of health professions education. Simulated patient examinations date back to the early 1960's, pioneered by Howard Barrows (Barrows and Abrahamson, 1964), with the term "standardized patient" credited to Geoff Norman at McMaster University (Wallace, 1997). Some 30 years of research evidence now supports the validity of the standardized patient method and the many different facets of this testing modality (e.g., Anderson & Kassebaum, 1993).

Performance examinations can also utilize mechanical simulators. These range from single-task trainers that present heart sounds to students for identification or provide a "skin surface" for suturing to complex teaching-testing manikins such as Harvey® (Gordon, 1999) and high-fidelity human simulator models such as Sim-Man® (Laerdal) and the Human Patient Simulator® (METI).

Chapters 9 and 10 address the measurement issues and special problems of performance examinations, with a focus on standardized patients and other types of simulations.

Other Assessment Methods

This "miscellaneous" category includes many different types of assessments traditionally used in health professions education settings globally. These are methods such as the formal oral exam, the less formal bedside oral, portfolios of student experiences and work products, vivas (the so-called "long case" and "short case" assessments) and some other traditional variations. There are some strengths associated with these non-standardized assessment methods, but because of the pervasive subjectivity associated with such methods the threats to validity are strong. There are serious limitations and challenges to many of these methods, particularly for use in high-stakes assessment settings from which serious consequences are possible. Nonetheless there is a strong tradition supporting their use in many health professions settings, especially in the emerging world. Chapters 11 and 12 review these methods with an eye to their shortcomings and methods to enhance their validity.

Assessment Toolbox

There are many other ways to categorize and classify various assessment methods. In the United States, the Accreditation Council for Graduate Medical Education (ACGME) and the American Board of

Medical Specialties (ABMS) recently collaborated in a wide-ranging assessment project known as Outcomes Project (ACGME, 2000). The ACGME General Competencies are a product of this collaboration, mandating that residency training programs assess and document their residents' competence in six domains: Patient care, Medical knowledge, Practice-based learning and improvement, Interpersonal and communication skills, Professionalism, and Systems-based practice (ACGME, 2000). The Outcomes Project also produced a Toolbox of Assessment Methods (ACGME & ABMS, 2000), which describes thirteen methods that can be used to measure the six general competencies. This document is a handy summary of what is known about the strengths and limitations of each method for measuring various aspects of what might be called "competence" in health professions education. Both the Competencies and the Toolbox are sufficiently general to be useful in many different areas of health professions education, and at all levels of training. We recommend that you download these documents and become familiar with their content. Table 1.1 summarizes the thirteen assessment methods included in the Toolbox. Many of the methods noted in the Toolbox (Table 1.1) will be discussed at some depth in this book.

Instruction and Assessment

While the major focus of this book is on assessment, it is important to remember that assessment and instruction are intimately related. Teaching, learning, and assessment form a closed circle, with each entity tightly bound to the other. Assessments developed locally (as opposed to large-scale standardized testing) must be closely aligned with instruction, with adequate, timely, and meaningful feedback provided to learners wherever possible. Just as we provide students with many different types of learning experiences from classroom to clinic, we must also utilize multiple methods to assess their learning across competencies, from "knows" to "does." An exclusive reliance on a single method such as written tests will provide a skewed view of the student. Since assessment ultimately drives learning, judicious use of assessment methods at different levels of the Miller triangle can help

Table 1.1 ACGME Toolbox Assessment Methods (ACGME and ABMS, 2000)

Type of Assessment	Definition	Chapter
1. 360-Degree Evaluation	Rating forms completed by multiple evaluators, such as peers, patients, instructors	Chapter 8: Observational Assessment
2. Chart Stimulated Recall (CSR)	Standardized oral exam using examinees' written patient records	Chapter 11: Oral Examinations
3. Checklist Evaluations	Observational methods used to rate performance in real-world settings; generally "yes–no" items	Chapter 9: Performance Tests
4. Global Ratings	Ratings scales used to rate performance in real-world settings; generally scaled 0 or 1 to N	Chapter 9: Performance Tests
5. Objective Structured Clinical Exams (OSCEs)	Structured, standardized performance assessments, administered in sequential stations	Chapter 9: Performance Tests
6. Logs	Written records of procedures or cases completed	Chapter 12: Assessment Portfolios
7. Patient Surveys	Satisfaction questionnaires completed by patients or clients	Chapter 8: Observational Assessment
8. Portfolios	Systematic collections of educational products	Chapter 12: Assessment Portfolios
9. Record Review	Systematic review of written records by trained evaluators	Chapter 12: Assessment Portfolios
10. Simulations and Models	Low- to high-technology performance exams that closely match real-life	Chapter 10: Simulations
11. Standardized Oral Exam	Highly structured oral examinations in which examiners ask pre-defined questions, with model answers	Chapter 11: Oral Examinations
12. Standardized Patient Exam (SP)	Simulated patients, highly trained to portray specific cases and rate performance	Chapter 9: Performance Tests
13. Written Exam	Selected-response type tests of cognitive knowledge; constructed-response (essay) type tests of knowledge	Chapter 7: Written Tests

ensure that our students focus their learning in ways that are most valuable for their future practice.

Some Basic Terms and Definitions

As we begin this journey, some basic terms and definitions may be helpful.

The terms and concepts discussed here will be used throughout this book and will be important to many other topics in the book.

Assessment, Measurement, and Tests

The *Standards* (AERA, APA, & NCME, 1999) define "assessment" very broadly to include about any method, process, or procedure used to collect any type of information or data about people, objects or programs. The focus of this book is on the assessment of student learning, and not on the evaluation of educational programs or educational products. We use the term *assessment* to cover almost everything we do to measure the educational learning or progress of our students or other trainees. The term "measurement" refers to some type of quantification used as an assessment. *Measurement* implies the assignment of numbers, based on some systematic rules and specific assessment process. While the measurement process may include some types of qualitative assessment, the major emphasis in this book is on quantitative measurement.

A "test" is a specific type of assessment used to measure or quantify the achievement of specific learning objectives. The term *test* generally refers to a specific assessment method designed to elicit and measure specific cognitive behavior (in contrast to observation of day-to-day activity, in vivo). (*Test* is typically used to indicate a cognitive assessment, such as an achievement test in gross anatomy; *instrument* usually indicates a non-cognitive assessment, such as a psychological inventory.) The term "examination" is used synonymously with the term "test," although educational measurement professionals tend to prefer the term "test."

Types of Numbers

Since a book on assessment in the health professions must deal with quantitative matters and numbers, it seems appropriate to begin with a brief overview of the types of number scales commonly used. There are four basic types of number scales that will be familiar to many readers (e.g., Howell, 2002). The most basic number scale is the *nominal scale*, which uses numbers only as arbitrary symbols. Coding a questionnaire demographic question about gender as a nominal response such as 1 = Female and 2 = Male is an example of a nominal number scale. The numbers have no inherent meaning, only the arbitrary meaning assigned by the researcher. The key point is that we can do only very limited mathematical procedures, such as counting, on nominal numbers. We cannot legitimately compute averages for nominal numbers, since the average "score" has no meaning or interpretation.

An *ordinal* number has some inherent meaning, although at a very basic level. Ordinal numbers designate the order or the rank-order of the referent. For example, we can rank the height in meters of all students in an entering pharmacy class, designating the rank of 1 as the tallest student and the last number rank as the shortest student. The distance or interval between rank 4 and rank 5 is not necessarily the same as the distance between ranks 6 and 7, however. With ordinal numbers, we can compute averages or mean ranks, take the standard deviation of the distribution of ranks, and so on. In other words, ordinal numbers have some inherent meaning or interpretation and, therefore, summary statistics are useful and interpretable.

Interval numbers are a bit more sophisticated than ordinal numbers in that the distance between numbers is meaningful and is considered equal. This means that the meaning or interpretation associated with the score interval 50 to 60 (ten points) is the same as the interval or distance between scores 30 and 40. This is an important characteristic, since the interval nature of these numbers permits all types of statistical analyses, the full range of what are called parametric statistics.

A *ratio* scale of numbers is the most sophisticated number scale, but is rarely if ever possible to obtain in educational measurement or the